MERRY CHRISTMAS
to KEITH
DECEMBER 25, 1993
from BETH

Hope you don't think I'm trying to make
an Intellectual out of you...

One Frog Can Make a Difference
Kermit's Guide to Life in the '90s

by Kermit the Frog,
as told to Robert P. Riger

illustrated by Tom Payne

A MUPPET PRESS BOOK

POCKET BOOKS
New York   London   Toronto   Sydney   Tokyo   Singapore

This book is a work of fiction. Names, characters, places, and incidents are either products of the author's imagination or are used fictitiously. Any resemblance to actual events or locales or persons, living or dead, is entirely coincidental.

POCKET BOOKS, a division of Simon & Schuster Inc.
1230 Avenue of the Americas, New York, NY 10020

Library of Congress Catalog Card Number: 93-84536

ISBN: 0-671-88064-0

First Pocket Books hardcover printing November 1993

10 9 8 7 6 5 4 3 2 1

POCKET and colophon are registered trademarks of Simon & Schuster Inc.

"Rainbow Connection" by Paul Williams and Kenny Ascher, published by Jim Henson Productions, Inc. (ASCAP)

Jacket and book design by Michael Picón

Printed in the U.S.A.

Acknowledgments

This book is the result of so many people's hard work, it's hard to know where to begin my thank-yous. Let's start with Tom Payne, whose magic brush makes me look a lot better than I have in years, and Michael Picón, who made my words and Tom's images all come together.

Shame on Jane Leventhal, my favorite publisher, who couldn't say enough about the making of this book. And without Louise Gikow's expert editing (and diplomatic skills), I wouldn't have a voice, let alone much of a sense of humor. Nor would I look quite right without the eagle eye of Lauren Attinello. Other diligent folks who helped me out include: Isabel Miller, Laura Hawk, Francesca Olivieri, Jennifer Mittelstadt, Catherine Rocco, and Didi Charney; not to mention Craig Shemin, who came up with the title ages ago.

Lorraine Shanley and my agent, Constance Sayre, deserve medals for letting me sit around their office writing this. Thanks to Marjorie Madfis, who loaned me lots of books and ideas. Also to Maggie Chandler, who was a big help with research and a great early reader, and to her roommate Emily, who, with the help of the Museum of Natural History, taught me a lot about my frog and toad forebears. Philip Leventhal also made a big difference.

I'd have gone crazy without Tom Hagerty, Betsy Groban, Andrew Greer, Michael Connolly, Mark Lanoue, and especially Dick Piper, who all contributed invaluable ideas and moral support throughout.

It is absolutely true that without the funny and fierce support of my friend and editor at Pocket Books, Julie Rubenstein, this book would not exist. Nor would it have been published so well without the enthusiasm shown by every single person at Pocket who has come in contact with the project, including Liate Stehlik, Bill Grose, Gina Centrello, Jack Romanos, Tom Spain, Lynda Castillo, Irene Yuss, Cindy Ratzlaff, Kara Welsh, Donna O'Neill, and Olga Vezeris.

Lastly, I'd like to thank a bunch of cats who, oddly enough, have stuck their feline noses into the mix at every turn along the way and each made a difference: Hidey, Pokey, the late Puck and Kitty, Mishegas, Rachel, Sophie, Dakota, Orville and Wilbur, Snuggs, Stalker, Lila, and Shadow.

Oh, and lest I get a black eye, I should profoundly thank my book supplier extraordinaire and main muse—Miss Piggy.

For Jim Henson
—*Kermit the Frog*

For Eleanor Sanger
—*Robert P. Riger*

For John Howard Payne
—*Tom Payne*

Contents

A Frog for All Seasons

LET ME TELL YOU how this all got started:

Piggy—you remember Piggy, right? Well, a few years ago, she got into this big self-help thing, and she began buying lots of books about her inner life, her inner child's inner life, her past lives…stuff like that. But after just a few minutes of intense soul-searching, she decided she wasn't the one who needed the help.

I was.

According to Piggy, I lack the openness and sensitivity to have a good relationship with her. I also have a fear of commitment that is keeping us apart. (Between you and me, it's more like a fear of getting squished.)

Anyway, she started to buy me books, starting with that one about the men's movement—*Iron Something-or-Other*? It seems like she's given me hundreds of them, each one with some new name for what she thinks are my problems.

And reading them did get me thinking. If all these guys could publish these books and make the bestseller lists, why couldn't I? I mean, *Piggy* even published a bestselling guide to life! (Between you and me, ever since *Charlotte's Web*, pigs have been a little pushy.) Maybe it was time for a frog to try the pen instead of the sword. (Besides, I didn't think I could lift a sword.)

So I got out this old typewriter I had from the "Muppet Show" days and started to write.

It's all kind of simple: Just don't take yourself too seriously and don't listen to experts (including pigs), and you've pretty much got it. See what you think.

Finding the Tadpole Within

I HEAR THAT EVERYBODY is looking for his or her inner child these days. And it makes me wonder: What's inside a frog? Is there a wild child within? A magical pollywog? A tender tadpole longing to be rediscovered, hugged, freed from the walls that block and bind its creative, spontaneous, spunky, pole-vaulting self?

I think I'm reading too many of these self-help books.

I like being who I am—Kermit the Frog, plain, green, and simple. Besides, what if I did find that tadpole within? What if he wasn't the nice little teddy bear of an amphibian we're led to believe he is? What if he were an evil child out of a Stephen King book?

But, in the interest of science, I thought I'd try to locate the little guy. So I got one of those tapes that try to relax you and bring out your inner self. It said to find a photograph of yourself before you were eight years old, so I did. It's a little hard to pick me out, because there were so many of us around the pond that spring, but there I was, hanging back from the rest, swimming upstream even then.

To begin my "reparenting journey"—well, that's what the tape called it—I sat down on my favorite log. Breathing deeply like they told me to, I ambled in my mind, over twigs, leaves, and little stones, till I came to the edge of the swamp. I watched thousands of tadpoles darting below the surface. And, suddenly, there was Tad (that's what I called my inner child). I reached out my hand to him…to welcome him, to introduce him to a frog from his future—me.

Then I fell off the log.

That was it. I couldn't get the mood back. Anyway, I got the feeling that young Tad didn't want to hang out with me. I mean, it would take all the suspense out of life if you spent time with your future frog.

Kermit with his brothers & sisters – age 8 weeks

He says   *She says*

Seven Habits of Highly Effective Frogs

THIS WAS INSPIRED by a book on how to succeed in business while trying much too hard. I figured that a collection of my favorite frog fortune-cookie fortunes might be more useful.

1. A quick tongue doesn't get tangled. (Say *that* three times fast.)
2. Look before you leap.
3. The early frog catches the worm.
4. A hop in time saves nine.
5. He who croaks last croaks longest.
6. Always try to stay out of a pig's way.
7. Remember: A toad may be somebody's mother.

A Toad May Be Somebody's Mother

22

The Frog Prince Gets the Last Ribbit

ALL THESE MEN'S-MOVEMENT GUYS think there are deep inner truths to be found in *Grimm's Fairy Tales*. They take a nice story about a young prince who gets into trouble stealing the secret key from under his mother's pillow and make a religion out of it—not to mention a bestseller.

Frogs don't have to go to the library to find out the hidden meaning of "The Frog Prince." We live it every day.

Imagine going through your whole life terrified that women of all ages (and species) will pick you up and kiss you, just on the off chance that you're really a prince in frog's clothing. Sound good to you? Well, it isn't.

Why would I want to turn into a prince, anyway? Who wants to be blond, blue eyed, and live in some dark, dank castle where everybody drinks mead out of wooden goblets and eats wild boar with their hands? For one thing, I'm sort of a vegetarian (larvo/lacto).

Besides, in the original story, when the frog is sleeping on her pillow, before he is transformed by her kiss, the princess flies into a rage, picks up the poor frog, and throws him against the wall with all her might. *Ouch.* (Come to think of it, she sounds a lot like a pig I know.)

You'd think women would be a little more sensitive. After all, they're the ones who don't like being treated as objects. But then they turn around and do the same thing to men. I feel like a rabbit's foot. Don't walk under a ladder in case it really is bad luck, and feel free to pick up any little frog you see and plant a kiss on his face.

Remember how when Snoopy kissed her, Lucy used to say, "*Yecch.* Dog lips"?

Yecch. Princess lips.

French for Frogs

LET'S FACE IT. French is a tough language for frogs, even though some people think France is full of us.

A while ago, I was supposed to go there on a trip to Euro Disney, so I bought a little book called *30 Minutes to Speaking French Like a Frog*. But it was almost useless. It didn't have any Froglais in it at all. Imagine not conjugating the verb *to hop*!

So here, in the interest of all you frogs who are planning a trip abroad to search for your roots, is a quick course in amphibious French.

27

la grenouille
frog

le crapaud
toad

ribbette, ribbette
ribbit, ribbit

le têtard
tadpole

"Bonjour, Madame la grenouille."
"Good morning, Mrs. Frog."
"Bonjour, Monsieur la grenouille."
"Good morning, Mr. Frog."

*"Bien le bonjour,
Monsieur le crapaud!"*
"Top of the morning
to you, Mr. Toad!"

*"Qui a fait naître tous ces milliards
de têtards, quand même?"*
"Who the heck hatched
all these tadpoles, anyway?"

le nénuphar
water lily

*"Est-ce que vous avez une chambre
qui donne sur l'étang avec un
nénuphar privé?"*
"Do you have a room that looks
out onto the pond with a
private water lily?"

30

l'étang
pond

la mouche
fly

"*Le marais est toujours plus vert de l'autre côté.*"
"The swamp is always greener on the other side."

Be careful here. Le Marais is also the chic-est neighborhood in Paris (naturally, a former swamp).

Les faux amis d'une grenouille (**false cognates for frogs**):

French has at least four words that sound like the word for green (*vert*):

verre	*un vers*	*vers*	*ver*
glass	verse	toward	worm

This can lead to some interesting conversation:

"*Ce n'est pas facile d'être vert.*"
"It's not easy being green."

"*Ce n'est pas facile d'être un ver.*"
"It's not easy being a worm."

Getting this right is all in the tongue—a pronunciation thing that should be mastered early on unless you want the French to use you for bait.

One more false friend to watch out for:

jouer à saute-mouton
to play leapfrog

Directly translated, this means to play leapsheep. Don't ask me.
I just write them down.

The only verb you'll ever need:

to hop
*je saute, tu sautes, elle saute,
nous sautons, vous sautez,
ils sautent*

"Je saute, donc je suis."
"I hop, therefore I am."

"Un saut, saut, et un saut."
"A hop, skip, and a jump."

It loses a little in the translation.

34

This should get you through at least your first week in France. The key thing is to roll your tongue just so when speaking. Try it out first on one of those handsome street vendors in the *Place des Anciennes Grenouilles* by ordering *un sauterne* (a great little frog after-dinner wine) and a *croak monsieur*. It's easy to say, and I understand it tastes pretty good, too.

I'm Not an Amphibian American, I'm a Frog

I DON'T WANT to be disrespectful or anything, but I think calling us Amphibian Americans is going a little too far.

I guess I can see how if you were a salamander, Amphibian American would be a step up, but it seems to me you should call a toad a toad.

Now, insults are another thing. *Wart-boy*, for instance. Piggy called me that once when she got mad. I got mad right back and called her a few names myself—*pork rind* is the one I remember. The next thing I knew, I was flat on my back. And Piggy had decided that she wanted to be called a Porcine Americaine, thank vous very much.

It's enough to give a *frog* warts.

37

Frogs of Madison County

PIGGY SNUCK THIS BOOK into the pile. It's the story of this lonely Maureen O'Hara look-alike war bride who gets seduced by a handsome middle-aged photographer (who can't even develop his own film!) when she is left alone at her dusty farm for a sultry August week while her husband and kids go to show their prize pig at the fair.

I think Piggy identified with the heroine. I'm not sure if I'm supposed to be the husband or the photographer who loves her and leaves her.

In my opinion, that girl should have left her husband, ditched the photographer, moved to the city, and become a photographer herself—one who could develop her own film.

That's what I'd call a happy ending.

Green and Mean

LET'S FACE IT. I'm not the hippest guy you'll ever meet, but I've always been you-know-what.

Earth Days come and go, and I'm still here, green as the day is long, living a life dedicated to saving the planet.

As far as I can tell, the green guerrilla movement isn't saving eco-systems, it's creating whole new ones—only they are eco-bureaucracies. Have you tried recycling a soda can lately? You need a Ph.D. Maybe instead of recycling centers, they should be called recycling universities.

What bothers me about all this "Green is beautiful" stuff is that it's getting to be a lot like Christmas—you know, all merchandising and no meaning.

One thing that does have a lot of meaning, at least for frogs, anyway, is all this animal rights stuff. Fewer and fewer frogs are getting dissected in high schools around the country, which is fine with me. Talk about cereal killers—kids in this country used to be raised on cornflakes and frog experiments!

By the way, did you read that article? You know—the one about frogs being the canaries of the environment? (They used to take canaries down into the coal mines to warn the workers when the oxygen was getting low. When your canary died, you knew it was time to get out quick.) It turns out frogs act as barometers for the health of the earth. When we start to go, so goes the neighborhood.

Well, I just want to say one thing: It seems to me that if you wait until the frogs and toads have croaked their last to take some action, you've missed the point.

The Frogal Gourmet

IF I HAD TO SUM UP frog cuisine in a word, it would be *fresh*. Of course, most of us love a good, home-cooked meal. But usually we're one or two steps ahead of the farmers' market craze—we just eat it when we see it.

That's not to say that over the years, a few great recipes haven't been handed down from amphibian grandmothers to amphibian mothers (and now that men are in the kitchen, to a bullfrog or two as well). But it can be tough cooking in a frog household, what with the tads being vegetarians and we adults preferring things that buzz and squirm.

So I thought I'd collect a few of my favorite recipes for you. And here they are.

45

Amphibian Appetizers

Worms Wrapped in Steamed Lily-Pad Leaves

This is a hit at most parties as an hors d'oeuvre (traditional at frog weddings), but it also works as a way to begin a simple supper.

30 small lily-pad leaves, rinsed
¼ cup fresh pond scum
½ bunch scallions, finely diced
    Salt and pepper
30 earthworms, rinsed lightly in
    fresh water to remove the dirt

Steam leaves in a large skillet. Lay each leaf flat and coat with a thin layer of pond scum. Sprinkle diced scallion on top; salt and pepper to taste. Lay a worm snugly in the center. Roll the leaf closed and fold the ends over. Serve while leaves are still warm. Yield: 15 servings.

Dragonfly Cocktail

No fancy party is complete without this traditional dish.

1   bottle cocktail sauce
25 large dragonflies, washed (peel off the tough part of the
carapace, but be sure not to damage the wings)

Put sauce in a dish and arrange dragonflies along the edge
of a serving tray. Set in view of a few
hungry frogs, and the flies will be
gone in no time. Yield: 25 servings.

Light Pond Fare

Kermit's Own Lime Green Vinaigrette

Serve over your favorite local greens or use as a marinade for grubs, slugs, or other succulent bugs.

½ *cup olive oil*
¼ *cup lime vinegar*
  Juice of 2 limes
 1 *whole garlic clove, mashed*
½ *cup chopped curly parsley*

Mix oil, vinegar, and lime juice until well blended. Add garlic and parsley. Let sit for several minutes before serving.

Pasta with Algae Pesto and Sun-Dried Pond Slime

 1 *quart algae, strained and finely chopped*
½ *cup grated log bark*
 1 *cup virgin oil*
½ *cup Parmesan cheese*
 1 *box spaghetti*
½ *cup grade A Mississippi sun-dried pond slime*

Prepare pesto sauce first by mixing algae,
bark, oil, and cheese. Boil pasta until
just about done; drain. Mix in
pesto. Sprinkle sun-dried
pond slime on top as
a garnish. Yield: 40
servings.

The Only Main Dish Worth Serving

Black Flies à la Kermit

40 large black flies
 1 cup olive oil
½ cup green vinegar
    Juice of 1 lemon
 1 diced water-lily flower (use
    ¼ clove of garlic instead if
    you're away from the swamp)

For this, you'll need a grill with very
small slats. Marinate flies in oil, vinegar,
lemon, and lily-flower mixture. Bar-
becue for 30 seconds on each side and
serve immediately. Yield: 20 servings.

Swamp Dweller Desserts

Shoofly Pie

So named because this goopy, flypaper-colored mixture is a virtual fly magnet.

3 *eggs, well beaten*
2 *cups brown sugar*
½ *cup darkest molasses*
1 *premade pie shell from your freezer case*
   Bread crumbs and raisins

Mix together eggs, sugar, and molasses. Heat pie shell till brown. Spoon in sticky glop and top with bread crumbs and raisins. Bake at 350 degrees for 30 minutes. Place near the swamp, and watch 'em land. Yield: 75 servings.

Chocolate Mouche Fondue

This has nothing to do with chocolate pudding and everything to do with chocolate-covered flies.

2 *cups melted chocolate*
25 *green flies, fresh, plump, and luscious*

For this, you will need a fondue pot. Melt the chocolate till it simmers lightly. Dip each fly one at a time. Savor the moment. Yield: 10 servings.

Note: All yields are frog sized. To convert for humans, divide by 10; for pigs, divide by 20.

Someday, I'll tell you the secrets of my holiday favorites: Christmas log (*bûche de Noël*), stuffed roast beetle for Thanksgiving, and the New Year's Day rack of centipede with lemon and garlic that my mother used to make.

Mr. Frog Goes to Washington

WASN'T IT NICE that a frog like me could get invited to a presidential inauguration? The animal guest list is usually limited to first cats and dogs (many of whom have also gone on to write books. Is there a pattern here?).

Anyway, I'm told it was the first time a frog had showed up in Washington in years (much less attended a ball and sat on the first lady's shoulders in the newspapers the next day).

I have to tell you, I believed the president when he pledged to make all of America a better place for frogs to grow up in once again. It all goes to show you: With enough grass-roots support, you can get elected without the swamp developers' lobby.

What Color Is Your Lily Pad?

RECENTLY, I STARTED to think about getting out of show business. You know, toss out the greasepaint before I get stale. Then I wondered what I would do next—after this author stuff, that is.

So I got a bunch of those books on finding out who you really are. You know: Answer these seventy-five questions and reveal the hidden talent that will make you a fortune.

It turns out I'm an ESTP—that's Extroverted, Sensing, Thinking, and Perceiving. I'm not a worrier; I "enjoy whatever comes along." I'm "adaptable, tolerant, dislike long explanations," and am best with "real things that can be worked on, handled, taken apart, or put together."

Maybe I should become a plumber.

Waiter, There's No Fly in My Soup

WHEN I GO OUT to a nice restaurant, aside from a decent table (being short and green usually means that I get stuck in a corner near the kitchen), all I really want is to get a good hot bowl of broth with flies in it.

Or worms.

Or, sometimes, grubs in hot garlic, with some crisp French bread to sop up the sauce.

But, no, these days, with health departments being so strict, it's virtually impossible to get any of these ingredients to land near the kitchen…much less in your soup bowl. So, while some people bring their own artificial sweetener, I just bring my own flies.

59

Iron Frog; or, A Fly in the Belly

I HAVE TO ADMIT IT. I sort of liked the idea of all these men's groups around the country helping you get in touch with your lost father and other stuff like that—although my dad wasn't lost or anything. (In fact, he has a terrific sense of direction.) Plus, these days, I spend most of my time with people, pigs, and bears. I figured that searching for my primal frog might teach me something.

So last time I was back in the swamp, I though I'd start a male frogs' group. I mean, just ten other frogs about my age, meeting a couple of times a week to talk about whatever came up.

The first thing we did was read that book *Iron Whatchamacallit* by Robert Fly. Of course, I wouldn't normally trust a fly, but I thought maybe this stuff was food for thought…or is it thought from food?

Anyway, this Mr. Fly feels that fathers are always buzzing off, going on the road and leaving their male offspring, so these young males can't learn about manhood from their dads…and since males can't learn about manhood from their mothers, either, they have to figure out a way to teach each other.

Well, that might be true for flies. But as far as learning about how to be a frog goes, well, you learn how to be a frog by…um…being a frog. Either you can catch a fly or you can't. Either you can hop or you can't. I can't see that it has anything to do with girl frogs or boy frogs or who's got a job away from home or anything. Besides, if you can't catch a fly or hop pretty darn quick, you're not going to be a frog much longer, anyway—male or female. You're going to end up either starving to death or as some hungry old alligator's dinner.

By the way, my frog group didn't last too long. What really broke it up was all that bonding stuff. The first week, it was banging on drums, dancing around in a circle, chanting "Rana, rana." It was really embarrassing.

Anyway, do you think our male ancestors hopped around the swamps with bongos, trying to get in touch with their inner selves?

I doubt it. If they had, we probably wouldn't be here.

Frogs Who Hop with Women Who Run with Wolves but Can't Keep Up

HERE'S HOW THE BOOK GOES: A fleet-footed earth-mother commando woman runs through the woods, her long hair loose and flowing, her teeth bared, glinting white in the evening sun, hands flat against her sides, following the easy gallop of the lone black *wolfita*.

Can you imagine this *frogito* trying to catch up with *that*?

I guess I can thank the Froggess that Piggy isn't the type to go running through a forest with anyone, especially a she-wolf. She's a lot more likely to go strolling through Central Park looking for truffles. And, afterward, she'd probably end up at Las Lobas, that toney new wolf-bar on the Upper East Side.

I'm Okay, You're a Pig

I JUST FINISHED this book by Thomas Harris. (Not the Thomas Harris who wrote *The Silence of the Lambs*. I don't read horror novels. And I didn't see the movie, either. Some of my best friends are sheep.)

Anyway, this Thomas Harris book was about living your life feeling okay about yourself by analyzing your interpersonal "transactions."

It turns out that everything I do is determined by the effects of FPT—or the frog-pig-tadpole interplay. It seems that my tadpole is always trying to act out his nonverbal whims but is being infected by the prejudiced pig's opinions that are rising against the blocked-out analytic thoughts of the frog within.

Hey, I didn't write the book. I only read it.

Frogs in the Military

THE LAST THING I ever thought I'd be in favor of was the right for frogs to bear arms. After all, frogs are a pretty nonviolent species—assuming you're not a fly.

But whether my feet are flat has nothing to do with whether or not I can drive a submarine.

Besides, where do you guys think they got the idea for frogmen, the Green Berets, and amphibious transport?

From my great-uncle, General Douglas A. McAmphibian, that's who.

Out on a Log

I HAVE TO ADMIT I'VE never been too interested in history. My uncles used to tell us stories of the great pioneer frogs, how they crossed the country in covered wagons, how they used to have to hop twenty miles each day from the swamp to school, how chocolate-covered worms used to cost only a penny at the local store. But I was always too busy practicing my banjo and dreaming of breaking into show business to pay too much attention.

Then Piggy gave me that Shirley MacLaine book about something called trance channeling. You're supposed to be able to find out who you were in your past lives. Piggy was told she used to be Cleopatra, Elizabeth I, and Marie Curie—all at the same time.

My first question was, How can it be that all the folks who show up in everyone's past lives seem to be either rich or famous or both? I mean, I've never heard of anyone who was told, "Well, sorry, but in the fourteenth century, you were an extremely unattractive horse thief from a poor village in an ugly part of the country, who was hung up by the thumbs in a dark jail cell for seventeen years before you finally expired from some strange and unpleasant disease."

But I decided to keep an open mind. I contacted this channeling person (they all seem to come from the West Coast), and we scheduled a telephone channeling session.

Before we started, he told me about these prehistoric amphibian cave paintings that prove frogs even predate dinosaurs, which meant I may have had lots of past lives.

The first "astral spirit" he connected with was back in ancient Egypt. Apparently, I was the great-great-great-granduncle of the Egyptian frog goddess named Heket, who had something to do with having lots of babies. (Makes sense she would be a frog....)

A few hundred years later, it seems I was fly-fishing in the bulrushes along the Nile and happened to accidentally kick this basket over toward the pharaoh's palace. Apparently, this changed history. Later that century, I was guest of honor at this big, important plague in Egypt that millions of frogs attended. (There were also lots of flies and locusts around at the time. No wonder we all showed up.)

From there we jumped ship to China, where froggist monks evidently used to worship amphibian graven images by the millions.

Then the channeler told me I got woken up one winter in seventeen seventy-something while hibernating on the banks of the Delaware River by this nice guy with wooden teeth who asked me how to get to the other side. I must have given him good directions, the channeler said, because here we are.

Finally, the channeler started in on this Napoleon guy, and how I was one of his economic ministers in the early nineteenth century—me, a frog who can barely figure out how much to tip!

At that point, I politely hung up. It's always seemed to me that living one day at a time makes the most sense, anyway.

Especially if you want to be able to pay the phone bill.

75

Fly-fishing with Kermit

FLY-FISHING HAS BECOME a really popular sport these days, and I think that's just fine. I've been fly-fishing for years, and I find it extremely relaxing. Plus, it's a great way to catch those really juicy flies that skim the surface of the pond but always stay way out in the deep end.

That's because fish aren't the only ones that think those silly feathered things look like flies. Flies do, too. (If you've ever looked through one of those fly-eye kaleidoscopes, you know flies can't see too clearly.) It works like a charm. Flies hover over to check out my lure, and bingo—dinner.

Color Me Kermit

Summer: Sporty Kermit   Autumn: Natural Kermit

Winter: Dramatic Kermit   Spring: Classic Kermit

Next Up...
Talking Frogs Who Date Pigs

IT'S INCREDIBLE. These daytime talk-show booking agents call at least once a day asking if Piggy and I would be interested in appearing on their TV shows. I guess they think an hour about interphylum relationships would be a real crowd pleaser.

Maybe we should just accept one of their offers. After all, think how much easier it would be for other couples like us if we came forward and told our story. (Not that our relationship is exactly a bed of roses. Although, I guess if you count the thorns, it might be.)

81

BEFORE   AFTER

Diets Don't Work

THEY DON'T. Really. I'm a slightly plump green guy with skinny legs, and there isn't anything a diet can do about it.

Besides, do you know how many calories a day they recommend for the active male frog? Twenty. That about gets me through a light lunch.

I tried a liquid diet once—two months of three algae shakes a day and a bonus of two measly flies on Sundays. I never thought I could

actually turn greener than I am. I did lose weight, but a month later, I was back to my usual size.

Then there was that diet that promised you could eat all the mosquitoes you wanted and still lose eight ounces in two months. The problem was, even at a few hundred mosquitoes a day, I was starving…on top of all the itching.

The last diet I tried was a low-fat one. Low-fat equals low taste as far as I'm concerned. Not to mention the amount of math you had to do to figure the percentage of calories you were getting from fat. I'm terrible at math. Besides, the FDA hasn't started labeling flies yet.

But the biggest problem with a frog diet is that eating is a reflex for frogs. See or hear a low-flying object, and out comes the tongue. Plus, it's really difficult to tell if what's buzzing past you is low-calorie or high-calorie. By the time you can figure out if it's on your diet, it's on the other side of the swamp.

Talk About a Green Thumb

YES, I HAVE TWO OF THEM.

No, I have absolutely no talent for gardening.

I know gardening is popular these days, but what can I do? I grew up in a swamp, vegetation all around, with the thumbs to boot—and flowers wilt at the sight of me.

The only success I've ever had is with my Venus flytrap. But that presents a whole other problem:

Competition.

What's So Bad About Codependence?

YOU KNOW, I understand how it can be tough coming from a dysfunctional human family. But when you're a frog, the Norman Rockwell domestic ideal seems a long way off.

Think about it: I grew up in a swamp. I ate bugs and algae. And there wasn't much sitting around the dinner table with Mom and Dad discussing the evening news. Remember, in a frog family, sextuplets are considered only children. My mother laid three thousand of us in one week!

So does that mean my family was dysfunctional? According to the books it was. And according to the books, from dysfunctional families spring codependent frogs.

Now, in my dictionary, codependence is defined as "feeling responsible for other people" or "trying to please other people." Well, where I come from, that's known as common swamp courtesy, or homepond decency, or just plain the froggy thing to do.

I'm not knocking the idea of putting yourself first and doing what you think is fun and good for you. But if that were all we did, we'd all end up being alone. And that doesn't sound like any fun, does it?

Not to mention those twelve-hop programs, where they expect you to be jumping from lily pad to lily pad telling all your friends why you're so messed up.

By the way, one of those books explains codependence by using that old frog-kissing story. "Did you hear about the woman who kissed a frog? She was hoping it would turn into a prince. It didn't. She turned into a frog, too."

So what's so bad about that?

An Amphibian Nuclear Family

For Pigs Who Love Too Much

MAYBE I'M A TOAD for saying this, but things between Piggy and me are the way they are, and that's that. I mean, I like Piggy and all, but we're just friends. Really. End of story.

She always says I'm not willing to make a commitment, but who started this? Are we joining a book club? I just wish she'd stop waiting for me to change. I'm not going to, no matter what she does.

The worst part is that I end up feeling guilty. But I'm not trying to hurt her. I just don't think of her that way. If this so-called syndrome means "measuring your love by the depth of your torment," then I'm glad she has such a thick skin.

The Tao of Kermit

FOR INSTRUCTIONS ON HOW to live life one day at a time, you can't beat Taoism.

The way I read it, Taoism really means just being yourself…keeping on a steady track when everyone, and everything, around you is going crazy. Anyway, that's what I try to do…although sometimes it's hard, with Fozzie and the rest of the gang going off in twenty different directions.

My favorite part is the teaching that says to stay away from self-help for the sake of self-help…otherwise known as what you haven't read about won't hurt you.

Affirmations for Those Who Are Green

To be said twice daily, while maintaining eye contact with yourself in the mirror. (No giggling, please):

I am a wonderful frog (toad).
I am a handsome (beautiful) frog (toad).
I can eat as many flies as I want without
    gaining weight.
I may not be able to run with wolves,
    but I can sure hop with them.
Someday I'll find it,
    the rainbow connection—
    the lovers, the dreamers, and me.
It's easy being green.